~A BINGO BOOK~

South Carolina Bingo Book

COMPLETE BINGO GAME IN A BOOK

Written By Rebecca Stark

ISBN 978-0-87386-533-3

Educational Books 'n' Bingo

Printed in the U.S.A.

DIRECTIONS

INCLUDED:

List of Terms

Templates for Additional Terms and Clues

2 Clues per Term

30 Unique Bingo Cards

Markers

1. **Either cut apart the book or make copies of ALL the sheets. You might want to make an extra copy of the clue sheets to use for introduction and review. Keep the sheets in an envelope for easy reuse.**

2. Cut apart the call cards with terms and clues.

3. Pass out one bingo card per student. There are enough for a class of 30.

4. Pass out markers. You may cut apart the markers included in this book or use any other small items of your choice.

5. Decide whether or not you will require the entire card to be filled. Requiring the entire card to be filled provides a better review. However, if you have a short time to fill, you may prefer to have them do the just the border or some other format. Tell the class before you begin what is required.

6. There are 50 terms. Read the list before you begin. If there are any terms that have not been covered in class, you may want to read to the students the term and clues before you begin.

7. There is a blank space in the middle of each card. You can instruct the students to use it as a free space or you can write in answers to cover terms not included. Of course, in this case you would create your own clues. (Templates provided.)

8. Shuffle the cards and place them in a pile. Two or three clues are provided for each term. If you plan to play the game with the same group more than once, you might want to choose a different clue for each game. If not, you may choose to use more than one clue.

9. Be sure to keep the cards you have used for the present game in a separate pile. When a student calls, "Bingo," he or she will have to verify that the correct answers are on his or her card AND that the markers were placed in response to the proper questions. Pull out the cards that are on the student's card keeping them in the order they were used in the game. Read each clue as it was given and ask the student to identify the correct answer from his or her card.

10. If the student has the correct answers on the card AND has shown that they were marked in response to the *correct questions,* then that student is the winner and the game is over. If the student does not have the correct answers on the card OR he or she marked the answers in response to *the wrong questions,* then the game continues until there is a proper winner.

11. If you want to play again, reshuffle the cards and begin again.

Have fun!

TERMS

Antebellum

Blue Ridge

Border

Catawba

Charleston

Civil War

Climate

Coastal Plain

Columbia

Confederate States of America

Congaree

Cotton

Crop(s)

Counties

Cowpens

Executive Branch

Five Civilized Tribes

Flag

Fort Sumter

Georgetown

Indigo

Andrew Jackson

Judicial Branch

Lakes

Legislative Branch

Livestock

Lowcountry

Francis Marion

Motto

Colonel William Moultrie

North Carolina

Palmetto

Piedmont

Plantation(s)

Revolutionary War

Rice

River(s)

John Rutledge

Sandhills

Sassafras Mountain

Sea Islands

Secede

Spotted Salamander(s)

State(s)

Tires

Tobacco

Upcountry

White-tailed Deer

Wolf Spider(s)

Yellow Jessamine

I

South Carolina Bingo

Additional Terms

Choose as many additional terms as you would like and write them in the squares. Repeat each as desired.
Cut out the squares and randomly distribute them to the class.
Instruct the students to place their square on the center space of their card.

Clues for Additional Terms

Write three clues for each of your additional terms.

_____

1.

2.

3.

_____

1.

2.

3.

_____

1.

2.

3.

_____

1.

2.

3.

_____

1.

2.

3.

_____

1.

2.

3.

South Carolina Bingo

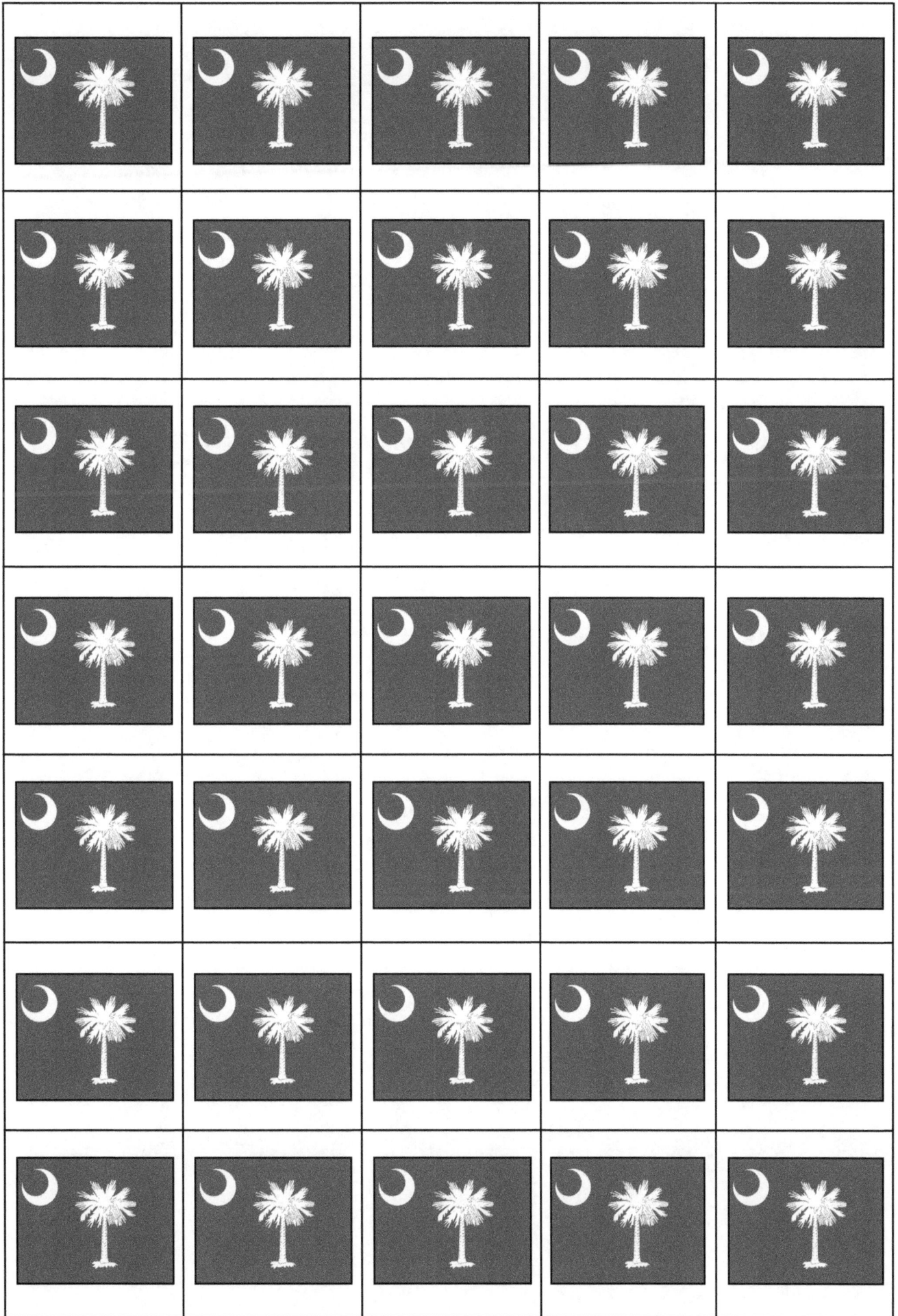

Antebellum 1. "___" generally refers to the period between the War of 1812 and the American Civil War. 2. The Boone Hall Plantation and Gardens is an ___ plantation in Mount Pleasant.	**Blue Ridge** 1. The ___ Mountains cover the northwestern corner of the state. The region makes up only 2% of the state's land area. 2. The ___ Mountains are the eastern part of the Appalachian System. Sassafras Mountain, the highest peak in the state, is in this region. It straddles the North Carolina border.
Border 1. Two states ___ South Carolina; they are Georgia and North Carolina. 2. The Atlantic Ocean forms the eastern ___ of the state.	**Catawba** 1. The ___ are a Siouan-speaking tribe. The tribe's reservation is along the border of North and South Carolina near Rock Hill. 2. The ___ Nation is the only federally recognized tribe in South Carolina today.
Charleston 1. ___ is the second largest city in the state. 2. The Siege of ___ took place from April 2 to May 12, 1780. This British were victorious and gained nearly complete control of the Southern colonies.	**Civil War** 1. These ___ battles were fought in South Carolina: the Battle of Charleston Harbor, the Battle of Fort Sumter, and the Battle of Port Royal. 2. The bombardment and surrender of Fort Sumter marked the beginning of the American ___.
Climate 1. South Carolina generally has a humid, subtropical ___, with hot summers and mild winters. 2. Factors affecting the state's ___ include its low latitude and elevation, its nearness to the warm Gulf Stream, and the Appalachian Mountains.	**Coastal Plain** 1. The Outer ___ extends about 70 miles inland from the coast. This flat area contains several rivers and swamps. 2. The Inner ___ consists of rolling hills and is very fertile.
Columbia 1. ___ is the capital and largest city of South Carolina. It is in the area generally known as the Midlands. 2. The official nickname of this city is "The Capital of Southern Hospitality."	**Confederate States of America** 1. South Carolina was the first state to secede from the Union and join the ___. 2. Jefferson Davis was President of the ___.

© **Barbara M. Peller**

Congaree
1. ___ National Park is the largest tract of old-growth, bottomland hardwood forest in the nation.
2. This national park has been designated a national natural landmark, a globally important bird area and an international biosphere reserve*.

an environmentally sensitive area with protected status in order to preserve natural ecological conditions

Cotton
1. Eli Whitney's invention of the ___ gin led to the explosion of ___ as a cash crop.
2. Between 1920 and 1922, the boll weevil caused ___ production in South Carolina to drop 70 percent.

Crop(s)
1. Agriculture is important to the economy. Important ___ include tobacco, greenhouse and nursery products, cotton lint, soybeans, corn, wheat, fresh tomatoes, and peaches.
2. Peaches are an important fruit ___. The peach is the state fruit.

Counties
1. There are 46 ___ in South Carolina.
2. ___ operate under four forms of government: council, council-supervisor, council-administrator, and council-manager.

Cowpens
1. The town of ___ derived its name from its original role as an overnight stop for cattle drovers.
2. The Battle of ___ was a turning point of the Revolutionary War; it was part of a chain of events leading to the Patriot victory at Yorktown.

Executive Branch
1. The ___ comprises the governor, the lieutenant governor, and several agencies in the governor's cabinet.
2. The governor is head of the ___. The present-day governor is [fill in].

Five Civilized Tribes
1. The ___ were native peoples of the Southeast. They included the Chickasaw, Choctaw, Creek, Seminole, and Cherokee.
2. The Indian Removal Act of 1830 authorized President Jackson to negotiate with the ___ for their removal to federal territory west of the Mississippi River. Some were removed by force.

Flag
1. The state ___ has a crescent and a Palmetto tree on a field of indigo blue.
2. The blue on the state ___ matches the color of the uniforms of Colonel Moultrie's soldiers; the crescent represents the symbol on their caps.

Fort Sumter
1. The first engagement of the Civil War took place here on April 12 and 13, 1861.
2. Confederate artillery opened fire on this Federal fort in Charleston Harbor on April 12, 1861. The fort surrendered the next day.

Georgetown
1. This seaport is the third oldest city in South Carolina after Charleston and Beaufort.
2. By 1840 the port of ___ was exporting more rice than any port in the world.

Indigo
1. Before the Revolutionary War, rice and ___ were important cash crops. ___ dye was sold to England where it was used in the textile industry.
2. ___ is the official state color. It was the color on the uniforms of Colonel Moultrie's soldiers and is the color of the field on the state flag.

Andrew Jackson
1. ___, the seventh President of the United States, was born in the Waxhaws border region of the Carolinas.
2. His nickname was Old Hickory.

Judicial Branch
1. The ___ of government interprets what our laws mean and makes decisions about the laws and those who break them.
2. The ___ is made up of several courts, the highest of which is the state Supreme Court.

Lakes
1. There are no large natural ___ in the state.
2. ___ have been created for hydroelectric power. The three largest are Marion, Moultrie, and Murray.

Legislative Branch
1. The General Assembly is the ___ of state government; it comprises the Senate and the House of Representatives.
2. The ___ makes the laws.

Livestock
1. ___ products are important sources of revenue; they include poultry products, cattle and calves, hogs, and dairy products.
2. Income from ___ mainly comes from poultry products, including broiler chickens, eggs, and turkey.

Lowcountry
1. The Atlantic Coastal Plain is also called ___.
2. Beaufort, Colleton, Hampton, and Jasper counties are in the cultural and geographic area called the ___.

Francis Marion
1. This Revolutionary War militia leader was born in Berkeley County. His nickname was the "Swamp Fox."
2. ___ led surprise attacks against the British, and was known for resourcefulness. He is often referred to as a "father of guerrilla warfare."

Motto
1. The ___ on the left side of the state seal is *"Animis Opibusque Parati,"* which is Latin for "Prepared in Mind and Resources."
2. The ___ on the right side of the state seal is *"Dum Spiro Spero,"* which is Latin for "While I Breathe, I Hope."

Colonel William Moultrie
1. ___ was victorious at the Battle of Fort Sullivan. The fort was renamed in his honor.
2. ___'s defense of the small fort on Sullivan's Island during the American Revolution prevented the British from taking Charleston.

North Carolina	**Palmetto**
1. ___ and South Carolina were one colony until 1729. 2. The Province of South Carolina was separated from the Province of ___ in 1729.	1. South Carolina's nickname is the "___ State." 2. The ___ is South Carolina's official state tree. It appears on the state seal.

Piedmont	**Plantation(s)**
1. The ___ Region is northwest of the Atlantic Coastal Plain. This gently rolling region gets hillier in the west. 2. At the southeastern edge of the ___ is the fall line, where rivers drop to the coastal plain. This was an important early source of water power.	1. ___ were large farms on which most of the work was done by slaves. 2. The main focus of a ___ was the production of a cash crop, such as rice or cotton.

Revolutionary War	**Rice**
1. More than 200 ___ battles were fought in the Colony of South Carolina—more than in any other state. 2. The Siege of Charleston, the Battle of Camden, the Battle of King's Mountain, and the Battle of Cowpens are a few of the many ___ battles fought in South Carolina.	1. Charleston and Georgetown grew into wealthy ports because of this crop. Mansfield Plantation is an antebellum ___ plantation. 2. Before the Revolutionary War, ___ and indigo were important cash crops. Their seasonal nature meant both crops could be grown with the same labor force.

River(s)	**John Rutledge**
1. The Santee, Pee Dee, and Savannah are major ___ in the state. 2. The Savannah ___ forms most of the border between South Carolina and Georgia.	1. ___ was the first governor of South Carolina after the signing of the Declaration of Independence. 2. ___ became the second Chief Justice of the Supreme Court of the United States when John Jay resigned.

Sandhills	**Sassafras Mountain**
1. The area known as the ___ divides the Atlantic Coastal Plain and the Piedmont. 2. The ___ is a strip of sand dunes on the western edge of the Atlantic Coastal Plain. These sand hills are evidence that this may have once been the eastern coast of the state.	1. At 3,533 feet, ___ is the highest point in the state. 2. ___, the highest point in South Carolina, is located in Pickens County in the Blue Ridge Region.

South Carolina Bingo

Sea Islands 1. The ___ are a chain of tidal and barrier islands off the coast. They are included in the Atlantic Coastal Plain. 2. Hilton Head is in the chain of barrier islands known as the ___ .	**Secede** 1. To ___ is to withdraw formally from an alliance or association. 2. On December 20, 1860, South Carolina became the first state to ___ from the Union.
Spotted Salamander(s) 1. The ___ is the state amphibian. 2. ___ spend most of their adult lives in underground burrows. They lay their eggs in a pool or pond.	**State(s)** 1. South Carolina was one of the 13 original ___. 2. When South Carolina ratified the Constitution on May 23, 1788, it became the eighth ___.
Tires 1. South Carolina is a leading manufacturer and exporter of ___. 2. Michelin, Continental, and Bridgestone are three major companies making South Carolina a leading producer and exporter of ___.	**Tobacco** 1. ___ is grown mainly in the Pee Dee region of the state. The South Carolina ___ Museum is in Mullins. 2. ___ is the leading crop and accounts for almost 25% of all income from crops.
Upcountry 1. The Piedmont and the Blue Ridge regions are also called ___. 2. In the late 1700s, the ___ of South Carolina was the American frontier.	**White-tailed Deer** 1. The ___ is the state animal. 2. ___ are able to run up to 40 miles per hour, jump 9 foot fences, and swim 13 miles per hour.
Wolf Spider(s) 1. The Carolina ___ is an official state symbol. It gets its name because it runs down its prey instead of trapping it in a web. 2. The Carolina ___ grows to 3 to 4 inches. Like other ___, it has eight eyes that are arranged in three rows.	**Yellow Jessamine** 1. The ___, the state flower, is found in every county. 2. Its funnel-shaped flowers are beautiful and fragrant, but poisonous.

South Carolina Bingo

South Carolina Bingo

John Rutledge	Antebellum	Border	Fort Sumter	Charleston
Executive Branch	Blue Ridge	Yellow Jessamine	Colonel William Moultrie	Spotted Salamander(s)
White-tailed Deer	Motto		Revolutionary War	Indigo
Upcountry	Sea Islands	Wolf Spider(s)	Francis Marion	Palmetto
Plantation(s)	Andrew Jackson	Crop(s)	Tires	Legislative Branch

South Carolina Bingo

Upcountry	White-tailed Deer	Lakes	Sandhills	Lowcountry
Palmetto	Counties	Climate	Sea Islands	Piedmont
Columbia	Andrew Jackson		Judicial Branch	Wolf Spider(s)
Rice	River(s)	Motto	Secede	Charleston
Spotted Salamander(s)	Yellow Jessamine	Crop(s)	Executive Branch	Tires

South Carolina Bingo

Andrew Jackson	Wolf Spider(s)	Counties	Francis Marion	White-tailed Deer
Palmetto	Blue Ridge	Coastal Plain	Antebellum	Sassafras Mountain
Sea Islands	Yellow Jessamine		Piedmont	Catawba
Motto	Columbia	Plantation(s)	Rice	Lakes
Tires	Confederate States of America	Crop(s)	Secede	Lowcountry

South Carolina Bingo

Motto	Piedmont	Border	Confederate States of America	Lowcountry
North Carolina	Civil War	Antebellum	Sandhills	White-tailed Deer
Revolutionary War	Rice		Legislative Branch	Fort Sumter
Wolf Spider(s)	Blue Ridge	Yellow Jessamine	Crop(s)	Climate
Congaree	Spotted Salamander(s)	Five Civilized Tribes	Tires	Indigo

South Carolina Bingo

Spotted Salamander(s)	Charleston	Sea Islands	Climate	Confederate States of America
North Carolina	Wolf Spider(s)	Coastal Plain	Judicial Branch	Blue Ridge
Border	Indigo		Colonel William Moultrie	Georgetown
Legislative Branch	Lowcountry	John Rutledge	Secede	Cotton
Counties	Crop(s)	White-tailed Deer	Motto	Revolutionary War

South Carolina Bingo: Card No. 5

© Barbara M. Peller

South Carolina Bingo

Catawba	Piedmont	Lakes	Lowcountry	Indigo
Francis Marion	Sea Islands	Cotton	Antebellum	White-tailed Deer
Sandhills	Congaree		Civil War	Judicial Branch
Crop(s)	Plantation(s)	Secede	Five Civilized Tribes	Border
Palmetto	Climate	John Rutledge	Revolutionary War	Cowpens

South Carolina Bingo: Card No. 6

South Carolina Bingo

John Rutledge	Piedmont	Georgetown	Wolf Spider(s)	Counties
Palmetto	Lowcountry	Andrew Jackson	Blue Ridge	North Carolina
Indigo	Fort Sumter		Judicial Branch	Civil War
Motto	Rice	Coastal Plain	Upcountry	Columbia
Crop(s)	Confederate States of America	Secede	Five Civilized Tribes	Catawba

South Carolina Bingo

Revolutionary War	Piedmont	Flag	Francis Marion	Civil War
North Carolina	Border	Sandhills	Indigo	Climate
Cowpens	Confederate States of America		Lowcountry	Charleston
Tires	Motto	Upcountry	Congaree	Rice
Yellow Jessamine	Crop(s)	Five Civilized Tribes	Sea Islands	Palmetto

South Carolina Bingo

Judicial Branch	Counties	Andrew Jackson	Cowpens	Confederate States of America
Congaree	Lowcountry	Revolutionary War	Sea Islands	Piedmont
Sassafras Mountain	John Rutledge		Blue Ridge	Flag
Cotton	Charleston	Plantation(s)	Colonel William Moultrie	Georgetown
Rice	Secede	Coastal Plain	Upcountry	Legislative Branch

South Carolina Bingo: Card No. 9

South Carolina Bingo

Upcountry	Francis Marion	Civil War	Sandhills	Cowpens
Indigo	Climate	Antebellum	Blue Ridge	Lowcountry
Confederate States of America	Piedmont		Fort Sumter	Columbia
Plantation(s)	Legislative Branch	Cotton	Secede	Sassafras Mountain
Coastal Plain	Palmetto	Lakes	Spotted Salamander(s)	Revolutionary War

South Carolina Bingo

Catawba	Piedmont	Sea Islands	Cotton	Palmetto
Flag	Sassafras Mountain	Colonel William Moultrie	Judicial Branch	Antebellum
North Carolina	Lowcountry		Lakes	Andrew Jackson
Coastal Plain	White-tailed Deer	Secede	Confederate States of America	Upcountry
Congaree	Crop(s)	John Rutledge	Five Civilized Tribes	Counties

South Carolina Bingo

Counties	Charleston	Sassafras Mountain	Francis Marion	Judicial Branch
Andrew Jackson	Palmetto	Border	Five Civilized Tribes	Blue Ridge
John Rutledge	Georgetown		Indigo	Sandhills
Crop(s)	Rice	Lowcountry	Upcountry	North Carolina
Piedmont	Flag	Confederate States of America	Congaree	Climate

South Carolina Bingo: Card No. 12

© Barbara M. Peller

South Carolina Bingo

Cotton	Charleston	Catawba	Sassafras Mountain	Indigo
Border	Flag	Lowcountry	Judicial Branch	Columbia
Francis Marion	Climate		Andrew Jackson	Georgetown
Revolutionary War	Secede	Civil War	Confederate States of America	Upcountry
Crop(s)	Legislative Branch	Five Civilized Tribes	John Rutledge	Colonel William Moultrie

South Carolina Bingo: Card No. 13

South Carolina Bingo

Executive Branch	Lowcountry	Sea Islands	Judicial Branch	Congaree
Climate	John Rutledge	Sassafras Mountain	Blue Ridge	Piedmont
Cotton	Fort Sumter		Lakes	Coastal Plain
Legislative Branch	Secede	Confederate States of America	Civil War	Catawba
Crop(s)	Sandhills	Columbia	Palmetto	Revolutionary War

South Carolina Bingo

Colonel William Moultrie	Judicial Branch	Sea Islands	Counties	Francis Marion
Catawba	Lakes	Antebellum	Border	Congaree
Indigo	John Rutledge		White-tailed Deer	Piedmont
Crop(s)	Sassafras Mountain	Flag	Secede	Cotton
Palmetto	Rice	Five Civilized Tribes	Cowpens	Andrew Jackson

South Carolina Bingo

Civil War	Sassafras Mountain	Flag	Cowpens	River(s)
Sandhills	Columbia	Georgetown	North Carolina	Fort Sumter
Cotton	Charleston		Indigo	Andrew Jackson
Motto	Climate	Crop(s)	Colonel William Moultrie	Upcountry
Congaree	Tobacco	Five Civilized Tribes	Rice	Piedmont

South Carolina Bingo: Card No. 16

South Carolina Bingo

Coastal Plain	State(s)	Livestock	Sassafras Mountain	Executive Branch
Colonel William Moultrie	Congaree	Secede	Fort Sumter	Georgetown
Judicial Branch	Revolutionary War		Tobacco	Flag
Legislative Branch	Palmetto	Upcountry	Sea Islands	Columbia
Plantation(s)	Cotton	Counties	Francis Marion	Charleston

© Barbara M. Peller

South Carolina Bingo

Cowpens	Confederate States of America	Climate	Cotton	Sandhills
Piedmont	Coastal Plain	Plantation(s)	Indigo	Congaree
Judicial Branch	Columbia		Livestock	Border
Charleston	Antebellum	Secede	Upcountry	Lakes
Tobacco	Sassafras Mountain	Sea Islands	State(s)	Catawba

South Carolina Bingo

Indigo	Catawba	Sassafras Mountain	Flag	Upcountry
Colonel William Moultrie	Francis Marion	Piedmont	Counties	Fort Sumter
State(s)	Confederate States of America		Blue Ridge	White-tailed Deer
Lakes	Tobacco	Plantation(s)	Rice	Livestock
Border	River(s)	Palmetto	Revolutionary War	Five Civilized Tribes

South Carolina Bingo

Executive Branch	State(s)	Francis Marion	Sassafras Mountain	Five Civilized Tribes
Climate	Andrew Jackson	North Carolina	Plantation(s)	Sandhills
Charleston	Georgetown		Motto	Antebellum
Spotted Salamander(s)	Yellow Jessamine	Tires	Rice	Tobacco
Wolf Spider(s)	Revolutionary War	River(s)	Upcountry	Livestock

South Carolina Bingo

Colonel William Moultrie	Catawba	North Carolina	Sassafras Mountain	Spotted Salamander(s)
Charleston	Livestock	Civil War	Flag	John Rutledge
Columbia	Palmetto		State(s)	Sea Islands
Plantation(s)	Counties	Tobacco	Legislative Branch	Revolutionary War
Motto	River(s)	Five Civilized Tribes	Coastal Plain	Rice

South Carolina
Bingo

English Schumacher?	Sassafras Mountain	North Carolina	Catawba	General William Moultrie
John Rutledge	Flag	Civil War	Livestock	Charleston
Sea Islands	State(s)		Palmetto	Columbia
Revolutionary War	Legislative Branch	Tobacco	Counties	Plantations
Rifle	Coastal Plain	Five Civilized Tribes	River(s)	Motto

South Carolina Bingo

Cowpens	Lakes	Livestock	Border	Cotton
Sandhills	Francis Marion	White-tailed Deer	Flag	Blue Ridge
Climate	Fort Sumter		John Rutledge	Georgetown
Tobacco	Legislative Branch	Rice	Antebellum	North Carolina
River(s)	Coastal Plain	State(s)	Columbia	Motto

South Carolina Bingo

Civil War	State(s)	Counties	Border	Five Civilized Tribes
Catawba	Executive Branch	Palmetto	Colonel William Moultrie	Antebellum
Lakes	Cotton		Tires	John Rutledge
Columbia	River(s)	Tobacco	Coastal Plain	Rice
Spotted Salamander(s)	Yellow Jessamine	Revolutionary War	Plantation(s)	Livestock

South Carolina Bingo

Five Civilized Tribes	Border	Counties	State(s)	Civil War
Antebellum	Colonel William Moultrie	Palmetto	Executive Branch	Catawba
Charno Rutledge	Tree		Cotton	Lakes
Rice	(Coastal Plain)	Tobacco	(Rivers)	Columbia
Livestock	Plantation(s)	Revolutionary War	Yellow Jessamine	Spotted Salamander(s)

South Carolina Bingo

Civil War	Revolutionary War	Executive Branch	State(s)	Flag
Livestock	Five Civilized Tribes	North Carolina	Sandhills	John Rutledge
Georgetown	Cowpens		Cotton	Columbia
Spotted Salamander(s)	Tires	Tobacco	Coastal Plain	Charleston
Wolf Spider(s)	Motto	River(s)	Francis Marion	Yellow Jessamine

South Carolina Bingo

Motto	North Carolina	State(s)	Sea Islands	Livestock
Antebellum	Charleston	Colonel William Moultrie	Civil War	Blue Ridge
Legislative Branch	Flag		Tires	Tobacco
White-tailed Deer	Spotted Salamander(s)	Yellow Jessamine	River(s)	Fort Sumter
Five Civilized Tribes	Executive Branch	Climate	Congaree	Wolf Spider(s)

South Carolina
Bingo

Overfish	Sea Islands	State(?)	North Carolina	Biome
Blue Ridge	Civil War	Francis William Modjine	Charleston	Antebellum
Tobacco	Ilres		Fort	Legislative Branch
Fort Sumter	River(s)	Yellow Jessamine	Spotted Salamander(s)	White-tailed Deer
Wolf Spider(s)	Congaree	Climate	Executive Branch	Five Civilized Tribes

South Carolina Bingo

Livestock	State(s)	Lakes	Sandhills	Cowpens
Plantation(s)	Francis Marion	Flag	Executive Branch	Civil War
Legislative Branch	Tires		Fort Sumter	Motto
Coastal Plain	Border	Spotted Salamander(s)	River(s)	Tobacco
Georgetown	Congaree	Sea Islands	Yellow Jessamine	Wolf Spider(s)

South Carolina Bingo

Lakes	Climate	State(s)	Executive Branch	Andrew Jackson
Spotted Salamander(s)	Tires	Colonel William Moultrie	Tobacco	Blue Ridge
Secede	Yellow Jessamine		River(s)	Motto
Cowpens	Catawba	North Carolina	Wolf Spider(s)	Antebellum
Congaree	Fort Sumter	Livestock	White-tailed Deer	Georgetown

South Carolina Bingo

Lakes	Executive Branch	White-tailed Deer	State(s)	Civil War
Andrew Jackson	Livestock	Tires	Sandhills	Fort Sumter
Yellow Jessamine	Columbia		Georgetown	Plantation(s)
Upcountry	Cowpens	Palmetto	River(s)	Tobacco
Border	Judicial Branch	Congaree	Wolf Spider(s)	Spotted Salamander(s)

South Carolina Bingo

Livestock	Executive Branch	Cowpens	Colonel William Moultrie	Judicial Branch
Rice	Plantation(s)	North Carolina	Georgetown	White-tailed Deer
Legislative Branch	Tires		Blue Ridge	State(s)
Andrew Jackson	Spotted Salamander(s)	Lowcountry	River(s)	Tobacco
Civil War	Flag	Wolf Spider(s)	Catawba	Yellow Jessamine

South Carolina Bingo

Confederate States of America	State(s)	Sandhills	Judicial Branch	Tobacco
Antebellum	Executive Branch	Lakes	Fort Sumter	Blue Ridge
Legislative Branch	Cotton		Georgetown	North Carolina
Wolf Spider(s)	Catawba	Border	River(s)	Tires
Spotted Salamander(s)	Indigo	Yellow Jessamine	Livestock	White-tailed Deer

South Carolina Bingo: Card No. 30